GOD IS ENERGY. DO YOU BELIEVE?

Using Science, Evolution, Creation and Religion to explain our existence.

SEMISI PONE
BSc, MSc (Hons). Auckland.

EDUCATION

My brain was empty
Then I learned the ABC
My mind was blind
Then I learned designs
Now I can see
As far as Eternity…

From "Rhymes of an Aspiring Writer"
by Semisi Pone.

CONTENTS

Introduction

I want to write this book from my own perspective and experience. I am sure you do not want too many complicated scientific explanations and theories. I am putting forward my idea like a conversation with your neighbour. It will be easy to understand.

I will use the bible and some "universal truths" to explain what I believe is the ultimate destiny of man. Our existence cannot be purposeless as evolution proposes. Just a mistake in the scheme of things on our planet and the universe.

Universal truths are scientific theories which have a lot of evidence supporting it and accepted by everyone.

We are all fascinated by our own mortality, the origin of mankind, the universe, God, creation and what happens when we die. Most people go to Church and involve themselves in religious activities as preparation for their "after life". Saving themselves from the eternal fires of hell. Perhaps the red giant that the sun will become before its final demise. Maybe the expansion of the sun is the hell the bible is talking about.

In that case, no one will escape. The whole earth will be burned to ashes. The sun will grow into a red giant and collapse into a "white dwarf" or "black hole". Of course, it will take a long time. Nothing is quick in the universe, in man years.

Only energy will escape to space. It cannot be destroyed according to scientific laws.

"Energy cannot be created or destroyed. It can only be transformed from one form into another".

For example, it can be transferred from solar energy into heat energy or mechanical energy and so on. They are manifestations of energy. It is an abstract, calculable quantity associated with the physical processes.

I am hoping to make a good argument that man will escape the burning earth as an "Energy Being", indestructible energy, as proposed by scientists; and populate planets in other solar systems or maybe galaxies far, far away.

We cannot travel by spaceship they are too slow and perishable. The quickest spaceship on earth can only travel at about 20,000 km/hr.

Man can travel as an Energy Being at the speed of light or faster. Light travels through space at 300,000 km/second.

Man as an "Energy or Super Being" will exist like God. It is indestructible and last forever. There will be no beginning or end. Time and space will become irrelevant.

When you live forever, travelling to other solar systems, stars or galaxies is not a problem. You travel at 300,000 km/second, you have all the time in the universe to get there. One billion years will be just a moment. One billion kilometres will be just a "hop down the road".

It will be interesting if we can recover our "galactic" memory, perhaps we may find out where we have been before we populated earth. The planets where we have lived, the solar systems we populated, the galaxies we visited in our existence before earth. It will be the greatest story of all time.

Enjoy.

CHAPTER 1. CREATION

God said, "Let there be light". And it was done. God said, "Let there be a heaven and earth, land and seas and plants and animals". And it was done. God created everything that he thought was necessary for earth.

Then God saw his creation was not complete. Everything was there except somebody to rule over the earth. So he created man in his image, from the dust of the earth. The very first human being, Adam.

Adam lived happily in the Garden of Eden with all the animals and the plants but he was not happy. God saw Adam's unhappiness and he thought that perhaps he needs a companion. So he took a bone from his rib cage and created the first woman, Eve.

Adam and Eve lived happily in the Garden of Eden, with everything provided for them by God. But there was one tree that God forbid them to touch, the tree of "good and evil".

God said unto them, "You can have everything that is in the Garden of Eden, but do not eat from the tree of "good and evil", for the day you eat from it; you shall surely die".

Then one day the serpent saw how happy Adam and Eve were, he was jealous of Gods creation. So he decided to ruin their lives forever. He said to Eve, "Is it true that God forbid you from eating from that tree?".

Eve replied, "Yes. God told us we will die if we eat from that tree".

"God is not telling you the truth. He knows when you eat from that tree, you will become like him. You will become Gods, knowing good and evil", the serpent said.

One day Eve saw how juicy the fruit looked and how inviting it is, she decided to try it. Maybe the serpent was right. She took a fruit from it and bit into it. Then she gave it to Adam who also bit from the fruit.

Then God opened their eyes and they realise they are naked. They were ashamed. They ran and hid in the bushes. God called them. "Adam..... Eve.... did I not tell you not to eat from that tree? Did I not tell you that you will die if you eat from it? From now on you will have to sweat for your food and drink. From now on you shall bear children in pain and die and return to the dust of the earth. You are banished forever from the Garden of Eden".

God also punished the serpent. "You shall crawl on your stomach and eat dust forever", God said.

Adam and Eve ran away and lived as nomads, wandering the desert and feeding off its meager offerings. They learned to domesticate animals and plants. They also bore 2 children, Cain and Abel.

One day Cain and Abel went to their garden, each with offerings to God.

Abel chose the best animal from his farm for his offering. Cain chose the worst from his crops for his offering. God saw Cain's heart was not good and he did not accept his sacrifice. He accepted Abel's who had a good heart. Cain was outraged that God accepted his brothers offering instead of his, so he killed him.

God said to Cain, "You have murdered your brother in your jealousy. You are banished to wander the earth. You shall not return to your parents".

"But God, I might be killed by others if they find me", Cain protested.

"No I will mark your forehead, no one will touch you", God said.

Cain wandered the earth. The bible say that he met other people and had children. **It is a question as to where those people came from.**

Perhaps God created more people when he was disappointed with Adam and Eve? The bible does not say where they came from. Maybe God also created others.

Adam and Eve had a third child named Seth and younger children as well.

The story of creation is probably the most read and most debated of all time. All Christians around the world study it and try to explain the scriptures. I think it is straight forward. God created everything. That's it. That is creation. God spoke and it was done.

There are 39 books in the Bible's Old Testament. All of them put a little light on creation and how God interacts with man. The most common pattern is that God is revered by man. God will punish those who are sinful.

The laws of Moses or the 10 Commandments was the ultimate judge of all men, at least in the known world of that time.

The Bible's New Testament approaches the rules of engagement differently. In the books of Matthew, Mark, Luke and John, they tell of the birth and life of Jesus Christ. He was the son of God. He came to fulfill the prophesies of the Old Testament and to save mankind from their sins, probably the fault of Eve and Adam by eating the fruit of "good and evil".

Jesus said, "I am the way, the truth and the life. No one can come to the father but by me". Christians believe in heaven and hell. Heaven is where the father is or God.

Good people go to heaven after they die. It is like paradise.

Hell is where the bad people are sent. They burn in its eternal fires forever, gnashing their teeth and crying out for some water to cool their sinful tongues.

The whole of the New Testament revolve around the life and teachings of Jesus Christ and his 12 disciples.

In John 3:16, Jesus promised heaven to all the believers;

"For God so loved the world that he gave his only begotten son, that whoever believes in him; shall not perish but have everlasting life".

The essence of the Christian faith is acceptance of Jesus Christ as their saviour by asking him to live their lives through him. That is the faith that will ultimately take them to heaven and everlasting life.

In the 10 commandments, God imposes the "tooth for a tooth" law. It was very tough on the followers of Moses. Moses proposed killing your enemy.

However, Jesus changed it into "turning the other cheek" which was also very tough for his followers. If your enemies slap you in the face, give them the other cheek to slap as well. It was "submission" in a sense.

The 27 books of the New Testament follow the same teachings and extrapolate on the teachings of Christ.

It appears that Creation as we know it only ended in death, Adam and Eve's punishment.

Christ came to give man everlasting life. To save man from the punishment given to Adam and Eve.

A lot of people do not believe there is life after death. It seems that everything ends **"when dust returns to dust"**. So what is the purpose of being born, live for a few years, maybe 100 years, then die forever? The universe is billions of years old. To only live in 100 years out of those billions of years is like a spark in the scheme of things in the Universe. A spark is maybe too long, but there is nothing else to describe how insignificant that existence is. How purposeless and meaningless it is.

Christ proposed that we will live forever as Spirit Beings, as part of the Holy Ghost.

When you die, your earthly body decomposes and return to the dust. Your spirit returns to the Holy Ghost, to God, where it came from in the first place. Man's immortal soul.

In the fourth chapter on "Energy" I will try to link the Spiritual Being and the Energy Being to **"prove"** that it is one and the same thing. Perhaps the ancients knew more than they wrote down?

Creation and Christianity is very straight forward. All you have to do as a Christian is believe in Jesus Christ as your saviour and he will do the rest through the Holy Spirit.

It seems that Adam and Eve's original sin, of disobeying God, necessitates the action of Christ, to bring man back to God.

The concept of the Trinity; God the father, God the Son and the Holy Ghost are the three manifestations of God is central to Christian faith. Three persons in one God.

Man will ultimately live forever as part of the Holy Ghost. As a "Spirit Being". It is the crown jewel of Gods creation. That is what the bible mean by "everlasting life". This will be discussed further in Book 2 in Hindu belief, that man's ultimate goal in life is to return to the Cosmic Spirit.

You cannot live forever as a human being. The flesh will die and decompose, it is your spirit that will live forever according to the bible. That is the whole Christian faith in a sentence.

Christ came to earth to save that spirit from God's original punishment of Adam and Eve and bring it back to him.

CHAPTER 2. EVOLUTION

Scientists believe that mankind developed, through millions of years, from inanimate compounds. In the beginning when there was nothing but the "primordial soup" on the surface of the earth. Lighting strikes the compounds and fused them to become a "living cell". It behaved like a single celled animal and started to divide. Perhaps over millions of years, and through natural selection, a single celled animal arose from those inanimate compounds.

The cell evolved into simple animals and plants and gradually developed into more complex organisms through "selection".

Natural selection was proposed by British Scientist, Charles Darwin. In his day it was ridiculed, that man's ancestor was a monkey. Natural selection is the process where organisms which adapt or are more suited to the environment survive while the others die off. For example, if the cells can survive in the methane atmosphere of the original primordial soup, they will live. Those that cannot survive in the methane atmosphere will die. Survival of the fittest.

A more straightforward example would be, "If bald men are not accepted by women then they will not marry and the "baldness gene" will die off, because it's not wanted. The selection pressure is against baldness. The gene for baldness will die. It will not be passed on to later generations".

Another example is, "If all ugly women are not accepted by men. Their gene will die off because they will not reproduce and the gene for being ugly is not passed on".

To explain how this works, every man and woman have genes in their chromosomes that contains the information which dictate everything in their development. Almost like a computer programme controlling the internet for example.

When the sperm is passed to the woman, it fuses with the egg in her womb, then develop into a foetus. The foetus contains the same information from the mother (egg) and the father (sperm). It will develop according to the information received from its parents.

The way it looks, how tall he/she is, what coloured skin, hair, bald or not and so on.

Half of the genes are from the donor of the sperm or father. Half of the genes are from the mother's egg. If the father is not bald or does not have genes for baldness. None of his children or grandchildren will be bald. The gene for "baldness" is selected against and will die out or become "extinct". Sometimes the females or mothers carry the gene from their ancestors, but through "selection pressure" over generations it will be slowly "weeded out" by nature. That is what Natural Selection is.

The same process applies to any other gene, like ugliness, disability, intelligence, stupidity and so on.

Sometimes, it is the environment that ultimately affects the expression of a gene. For example, if an intelligent baby is born into a stupid society, he or she "learns" to be stupid until she moves to an "intelligent" society where her intelligence is expressed by learning from intelligent people around him or her.

A bit humorous but it clarifies the point.

Another example is skin colour. Sometimes brown parents have white children. It is because they carry the gene from their ancestors. They probably have white ancestors or Europeans who gave them the gene for white skin and a lot of other traits that may be "hidden" and expressed generations down the line.

The theory of evolution has become a lot more complicated since Charles Darwin. Scientists now study natural selection at the molecular level. At the chromosome and genetic level which ultimately explains why things are the way they are with living organisms.

In Darwin's day, it was the physical characteristics like different beak sizes in finches or the variety of shapes of flowers and so on. Now Scientists are studying why and how genes work. How does nature store that information inside the genes? And pass it on for millions of years? Computer programmes will not last that long.

Computer programmes are not as complicated or as vast as genetic information. A single gene contains information that can be stored in a lot of computers, maybe thousands. Yet you cannot see a gene, it is very, very, very small.

In summary, in the beginning when there was nothing on earth; just the primordial soup and a methane atmosphere, lightning hit some inanimate compounds and fused them to become the "first living cell". They behaved like living organisms and divided like a living cell.

Eventually over time and through natural selection, it developed into single then multi-celled organisms. It developed into complex organisms, then fish, then developed legs and lungs and invaded land. It developed into different types of animals, became a monkey then man. Similarly, other organisms, for example, fishes and plants evolved in the same way. It probably took billions of years. That is the theory of Evolution in 2 paragraphs.

CHAPTER 3. GOD

The concept of God is a very complex and difficult one to explain, even by Ministers of the Christian Churches. When I was young and used to attend Church every Sunday, we were told that God came from God. It was sufficient explanation in those days. As I grew older and went to school then University, I learned other theories like Evolution, for example. God became even bigger and more complex as I learned more.

Then I learned about the Universe and how vast it is, I became even more intrigued. Now God is so big, it's as large as the Universe itself or bigger.

To give you an idea of how large the Universe is, consider the nearest star to our sun or solar system. It is called by Scientists "Proxima Centauri". It is 4 light years away, from earth. A light year is the distance that light travels through space in one year.

Light travels at 300,000 km per second. In 1 year it will travel 9,500,000,000,000 kilometres. In 4 years, it would have travelled 38 billion kilometres. It is a huge number. Our fastest spaceship will take a long, long, long, long time to get there, 190,000 years at 20,000 kilometres per hour! There is no way we can travel anywhere in our spaceships.

Some stars are up to a thousand light years away from us! And that is just in our galaxy, the Milky Way which is 100,000 to 120,000 light years in diameter. There are other galaxies, in fact more than 170 billion galaxies, in the observable universe!. They maybe millions of light years away! It is mind boggling how vast the Universe is.

Scientists have pictures of those galaxies in your Science text books at school and encyclopedias like Wikipedia. You can look and read about them. It is such a fascinating subject.

If God created all of that, it is unimaginable how powerful God is. It is a bit difficult to think that everything including the creation of the Universe was just a mistake. Natural selection having the final word.

I propose that God is Energy. The whole earth is held together and made up of energy. The whole Universe is made up of energy. God is Energy. What holds the sun, solar system and galaxies in place? In the emptiness of space? They are not just floating! In fact they are moving at very fast speeds!

Our sun gives energy to plants which use it to make carbohydrates which sustain all other living organisms on Earth. The sugars in the carbohydrate releases the energy when digested by animals. Scientists say that this energy from the sun comes in electromagnetic waves or visible light. It is also proposed that these electromagnetic waves are absorbed, by plants, in packets called photons which behave like waves and also particles. It is called the wave-particle duality.

So light is made up of particles that flow like a wave. In this case, an electromagnetic wave. Energy may be stored inside those particles. Just a description of this kind of energy. Just like all other forms of energy, thermal, mechanical, heat, nuclear and so on. All manifestations of the same thing.

The Penguin Encyclopedia describes energy as *"an abstract calculable quantity associated with all physical processes and objects whose total value is conserved"*.

What they mean is that the total value of the energy is never lost. In other words, *"energy cannot be created or destroyed, only transformed from one form into another"*. For example, from thermal into mechanical then heat. Like steam powering a paddle boat on the Mississippi river. The steam turns the engine which turns the paddle. That is thermal energy; steam converted into mechanical energy moves the paddle. There is also heat generated by the friction between the paddle and the water, heat energy.

God is an enigma. No one really knows where God came from or how he operates. Or how he created the Universe. Scientists have a lot of theories about how the Universe started and how it continues to evolve and expand.

The Big Bang Theory is probably the most accepted.

However, according to the bible, in the beginning there was God and nothing else. The "word" was God. The word created everything. The word of God. Science and religion share this in common. They both agree that there was nothing in the beginning. Science believes that the "Big Bang" created the Universe. Religion believes that God created it.

Religion believes that God has 3 manifestations or the Trinity. God the father. God the Son and God the Holy Ghost.

God the father created the heavens and the earth. God the son came to earth to save mankind from the punishment of Adam and Eve, and their sins. When he returned to heaven he told his disciples he will sent them the "Holy Spirit" to guide them.

Christians believe that it is the Holy Spirit that guide us today. The Holy Ghost.

When we die, we either return to God or burn in the eternal fires of hell. It is our spirit that God claims. As he said to Adam and Eve, their bodies will die and return to the dust from where it came.

Christians propose that Jesus saved our spirit. God did not mention a spiritual being when he punished Adam and

Eve from the Garden of Eden. The King James version of the bible does mention that God said "they", probably the Trinity, will not allow Adam to eat from the fruit of eternal life and live forever like God.

God put an angel at the entrance to the Garden of Eden with a flaming sword to keep Adam and his descendants out of the Garden of Eden or they might eat from the fruit of eternal life and live forever.

So the idea of Eternal life came from God the Son, Jesus Christ as he promised in John 3:16.

"God so loved the world that he gave his only begotten son; that whoever believes in him shall not perish but have everlasting life".

God the Son, Jesus Christ, gave his earthly body to die for our sins; the reasons why Adam and Eve were punished in the first place, so we can return to God, so we can have eternal life, which was taken away from Adam and Eve for disobeying God.

When God the Son, Jesus Christ, returned to heaven he promised his disciples he will send the Holy Ghost to be their helper.

All believers have to do is to invite God the Holy Ghost to live inside them and change their lives. Being "Born Again", as it is called by Christians around the world. We see it all the time on the Evangelical TV Programmes, believers praying to God the Holy Ghost to enter their bodies and become one with them.

To cleanse them of their sins so they become a new person, just like being born as a baby. It is this new person that Jesus Christ came to resurrect from the dust that Adam and Eve were punished to forever, by God the Father. God the Son, Jesus Christ, gave man a chance to live forever by sending God the Holy Ghost to save him, just like God the father's original intention with Adam and Eve.

The mighty Roman Empire persecuted the Christians. They were killed or thrown to the lions for Roman entertainment. But to-day, the mighty Roman Empire is gone. Rome is now the center of the largest Christian church, the Catholic Church.

How did the Christians overcome the Roman Empire? They did not have a trained army like the Romans. They did not have the infrastructure and money to fund it.

The Christians only had the teachings of Christ to guide them. They also had a secret weapon that the Romans did not know about or understand how it works. A weapon so powerful it can heal the sick, move mountains and change the most fierce Roman soldier's hearts, the Holy Spirit. It was the weapon Jesus promised to send them. The bible described it as like a powerful wind that looked like tongues of fire which entered the disciples and empowered them to perform miracles in the name of Jesus.

Jesus had commanded his disciples to "go unto the world and make all men my disciples". It is still happening today. Now the Christians have 2-3 billion members, the largest religious group on earth. It is the power of the Holy Spirit that is driving it. The Christians "have inherited the earth". They control the world economy, its military, institutions and more....and they are still performing thousands of miracles everyday.

Scientific discoveries are made, the dead are raised in the hospitals everyday, they convert water into wine, fly in jet planes, manufacture miracle medicine and so on. It seems that man's powers come from the Holy Spirit. He can perform miracles and do things that were normally not part of his abilities.

I propose it is because we are all part of God. Our "immortal soul". The "Energy Being" or "Spirit" is the image of God within us. The Holy Spirit.

Science explains how our bodies breakdown the food we eat into energy to sustain our bodies. This energy then passes on into other forms of energy. It cannot be destroyed. When we die, our bodies decompose, but the energy that kept us going moves on to some other form.

Heat energy. Stored energy in microbes that decompose our bodies and so on.

Is that our spirit? That energy that leaves our body when we die? It can turn into anything or other forms.

Does it go back to space, heaven or enter a new body as in reincarnation? Our bodies cannot live without that energy. It comes from the food as explained by scientists. That energy in the food came from the sun in particles in the electromagnetic waves.

Science explains that in the sun's core there is an "eternal nuclear furnace" breaking down the "nuclear" fuel and giving off a small percentage of that energy as electromagnetic waves which reaches earth, and the plants trap and convert it into carbohydrates to sustain all living organisms on earth.

When those organisms die the energy moves on to other forms.

Is it God the Holy Ghost? Packaged in small amounts inside particles that are brought to earth by electromagnetic waves from the sun?

No one has been to the sun's core to see what is going on over there. All we have is the scientific theories to explain it. Is God inside the core of the sun? The bible says that God is "everywhere". Which means that God is part of everything. It is not limited to the sun only. The surface of the sun is just a molten, explosive eternal fire!

It is energy that drives the whole universe. That is one thing that is common to all parts of the Universe, Energy. So the bible may have explained God. God is everything. God is energy, it is everywhere. It is part of everything. It holds everything in place.

When energy is released from a small piece of nuclear fuel, it is so huge and explosive that the atom bomb is the result. It only happens when man discovers how to release it.

God cannot exist without some kind of consciousness or intelligence. Science has yet to explain why we have the intelligence that we have. We all have the same brain cells but some people are smarter than others. Monkeys are not as smart as humans yet their brains are about the same size.

God the Holy Ghost provides that "consciousness". That light that seem to go out of your eyes when you die. Your eyes become opaque and your body lifeless. That is intelligence that is part of all living things. We cannot explain it because our current knowledge and technologies is underdeveloped.

Is the Universe as a collective part of God the Holy Ghost, intelligent? It must be. Otherwise, why do things happen as they do? It cannot be just a galactic mistake!

Is our whole existence and the universe a mistake? As proposed by some people? Natural Selection is not a mistake! There is a definite design there! All living things evolve to become better or more adapted to their environment. That is a definite design. Otherwise, animal evolution will be moving in different directions with no pattern whatsoever. Mistakes in nature are random they are not in a pattern.

The concept of God is becoming clearer.

CHAPTER 4. ENERGY

Energy that gives us life comes from the sun. Scientists suggest that a small proportion of the energy generated in the sun's core travel to earth as electromagnetic waves. Packets of energy make up those electromagnetic waves....called photons, which behave like particles and a wave. The particle-wave duality.

This energy is trapped by the chlorophyll in plants and used to make sugars that sustain animals, fishes and other organisms that feed on those plants including man.

This energy is passed on from the plants to primary feeders or herbivores then carnivores and so on in the food chain. Man is ultimately the top of the food chain. When we eat our food, whether they be plant or animal products our bodies digest the food and the energy is released to power our muscles, nerves, skeletal structure so that we can carry out our normal activities.

There are also other sources of energy like wind energy which is used to turn turbines and generate electricity. There is also wave energy, hydro-energy, fossil energy from coal, oil and so on. In fact there are a large number of energy sources. The sun's rays can also be trapped as solar energy. They are all different manifestations of the same thing.

As mentioned in the previous paragraph the Penguin Encyclopedia describe energy as ***"an abstract calculable quantity associated with all physical processes and objects whose total value is conserved"***. This means the total value of the energy is never lost. It can only be transformed into another form. The whole world, both living and non-living are affected by energy in one form or another. Some energy from the sun may be lost into space or transformed into carbohydrates, or mechanical energy but the total will always be the same.

Sometime in the future, the sun will expand as it runs out of fuel in its core and earth will be burned to ashes. Energy will be transformed into another form, maybe heat and escape into space. To explain this in more detail, according to scientists, when stars run out of fuel, they expand into a "red giant". Our sun which is 1.2 million kilometres in diameter will expand into 100 million kilometres in diameter or bigger.

The earth is 150 million kilometres from the sun. When the sun expands, it will be 100 million kilometres nearer to earth, its surface temperature will increase by a factor of 100,000s. In the core it is 15 million degrees centigrade. On the earth it may be more than 100,000 degrees centigrade on the surface. Not only from the sun being nearer, but also from the increased heat on its surface and brightness. That heat is probably enough to melt and turn the earth into ash, the other closer planets as well.

This is what the online encyclopedia Wikipedia explains...

In about 5 to 6 billion years, the Sun will have depleted the hydrogen fuel in its core and will begin to expand. At its largest, its surface will approximately reach the current orbit of the Earth. It will then lose its atmosphere completely; its outer layers forming aplanetary nebula and the core a white dwarf. The evolution of the Sun into and through the red-giant phase has been extensively modelled, but it remains unclear whether the Earth will be engulfed by the Sun or will continue in orbit. The uncertainty arises in part because as the Sun burns hydrogen, it loses mass causing the Earth (and all planets) to orbit farther away. There are also significant uncertainties in calculating the orbits of the planets over the next 5 – 6.5 billion years, so the fate of the Earth is not well understood. At its brightest, the red-giant Sun will be several thousand times more luminous than today but its surface will be at about half the temperature. In its red giant phase, the Sun will be so bright that any water on Earth will boil away into space, leaving our planet unable to support life.

Mercury, Venus, Earth and Mars will turn into ash or thrown into outer space. The other planets Jupiter, Saturn, Uranus, Neptune and Pluto may be affected as well but they are a bit further away from the sun. As gas planets, they might just evaporate into space.

Red Giants are often described as "cool", but that is probably in relation to other stars which may be hotter.

The sun will ultimately collapse after its initial expansion. If the speed of collapse is faster than the speed of light, 300,000 kilometres per second, it will turn into a "black hole" with nothing escaping out of it. Not even light. Otherwise it will turn into a "white dwarf" which is no bigger than earth, only about 12,000 kilometres across instead of 1.2 million kilometres across.

The planets that are still orbiting the sun will probably be flung into space as its gravitational pull is no longer enough to hold them in place. Forces on them might be enough to break them apart into asteroids or perhaps turn them into "wandering comets". Attracted by the gravitational pull of distant stars or just evaporate.

The energy which has held our solar system together will probably "escape" into space or transformed into another form. The energy that was once part of us, keeping us alive, moving and operating will probably escape into space as well as heat, after the sun's heat burn our earthly bodies to ashes. Where does all the energy go?.

Do they just form a wave and travel at the speed of light to be captured by distant stars, plants and so on? The energy that was once part of us is transformed into packets of photons , wandering aimlessly in space until captured by the gravity of other solar systems and attracted to their living beings?.

It seems a bit chaotic and accidental.

The Universe is a very orderly place with everything in a pattern, proof of intelligent intervention. God's Creation.

Suppose God is energy, God is part of everything. Christians believe God is "everywhere". If God is energy, this belief will be true.

Energy is everywhere, it holds everything in the universe together. From huge galaxies millions of light years across to tiny atoms that we cannot even see with our most powerful electron microscope. This energy is so great that when released, like in an atomic bomb, it has colossal destructive power. The energy that holds the atom together.

Does energy have "consciousness"? Like a living being? It seems to be present everywhere, cannot be destroyed and transformed into one form or another. Scientists still cannot explain it.

Are "spirit beings" made of energy? There has been numerous reports of "ghosts" and "spirits" from all parts of the globe. Are they "Energy Beings" which have left their human form? The energy that was once driving the human body is now existing by itself as a "Spirit"?

Christians believe that when we die our spirits goes back to God. It may vary between different Churches and religions, but the principle is still the same.

When humans die their spirits go to God, the Cosmic Spirit or heaven, paradise and so on. No one has bothered to explain "spirits" in scientific terms. Probably from the lack of evidence, but if billions of people believe it, for 2,000 or more years now; there must be something in it. It may be that in order to "see" the evidence scientist may have to look at this proposal from another angle. The spiritual angle.

If energy does have "consciousness", it may be possible for energy beings to exist, in whatever form as dictated by its environment. It will solve a lot of problems like time and space travel as energy beings are indestructible.

This is how wikipedia explains energy...

In physics, **energy** is a property of objects, transferable among them via fundamental interactions, which can be converted into different forms but not created or destroyed. The joule is the SI unit of energy, based on the amount transferred to an object by the mechanical work of moving it 1 metre against a force of 1 newton.

Work and heat are two categories of processes or mechanisms that can transfer a given amount of energy. The second law of thermodynamics limits the amount of work that can be performed by energy that is obtained via a heating process—**some energy is always lost as waste heat**. The maximum amount that can go into work is called the **available energy**. Systems such as machines and living things often require available energy, not just any energy. Mechanical and other forms of energy can be transformed in the other direction into thermal energy without such limitations.

There are many forms of energy. Common energy forms include the **kinetic energy** of a moving object, the **radiant energy** carried by light and other electromagnetic radiation, the **potential energy** stored by virtue of the position of an object in a force field such as a gravitational, electric ormagnetic field, and the **thermal energy** comprising the microscopic kinetic and potential energies of the disordered motions of the particles making up matter. Some specific forms of potential energy include elastic energy due to the stretching or deformation of solid objects and **chemical energy** such as is released when a fuel burns. Any object that has mass when stationary, such as a piece of ordinary matter, is said to have rest mass, or an equivalent amount of energy whose form is called **rest energy**, though this isn't immediately apparent in everyday phenomena described by classical physics.

CHAPTER 5. THE ENERGY BEING

I have thought about the idea of man as a spirit for a long time, ever since I started going to Sunday school in our local Methodist Church as a child. Christians believe, and it is written in the bible, that there is life after death. When our earth bodies die and decompose, it returns to the earth…it becomes one with the earth. Dust return to dust as God said to Adam. But man's spirit lives on forever. It is this spirit that is a bit of an enigma, there is very little we know about man's spirit being. We know it lives inside us but that is about all. I would like to discuss the Spirit or Energy Being in more detail in this chapter.

There are several concepts or ideas that all refer to the Energy Being or the Spirit. In modern teachings of many "enlightened" people…it is referred to as the "inner self" or your "inner voice "or your "gut feeling" or "instinct" or "mind" or "soul". We always refer to it as if it is somebody else inside us who actually make some decisions for us. We feel it like a gut feeling, intuition, inner voice and so on. Sometimes we act on it sometimes we don't. It is how Christians live by "listening to God". But no one has ever pointed out that all those concepts or ideas are all referring to the one and same thing. The Spirit or Energy Being inside all of us.

It is my view that the Spirit or Energy Being is the one who was made in the image of God. It is the all powerful person that performs miracles and is indestructible.

37

Because it is energy, it cannot be created or destroyed. It can take on many forms. It is intelligent and "all seeing". It knows everything and have power over everything. But how do we harness the power of that powerful indestructible being in us? How do we get it to do what we want?

When I was a salesman, one of the things that we were taught is called "affirmations". It is almost like meditation. Before entering somebody's house to make a presentation we were taught to perform an affirmation. It involves writing down the things you want to happen in that sales presentation and repeating it a hundred times or so to yourself before going into the house. You feel confident and focused on what you want from that presentation. The customer will also feel the power and conviction of your presentation and will be more likely to buy your product.

The same thing happens with missionaries when they preach to a group of non-believers. The listeners can feel the power of his convictions and faith and will want to join him and become a Christian. But who is the actual creator of that conversion? To make the sale? And to convert non-believers? Is it the Super Being inside us? The Energy Being? The Spirit? Are we just making the affirmations just like we are praying to him asking the Super Being to do things for us?

The power of prayer is well known amongst Christian believers. There are about 2-3 billion or more Christians on earth. They all believe in the power of prayer. When they pray they can feel the power of God, the presence of God amongst them. They feel peace. They feel blessed. They feel enlightened. They feel more powerful after prayer. Is it because they have awakened the Super Being inside them? The Spirit? When the Spirit or God takes over their lives and making decisions they do become like a super being themselves. They do things they normally would not do because they have faith in what they are doing. They believe that God will award them what they ask for. And it usually happens!

When I was a child going to Sunday school in our local Methodist Church in Tonga, I was brought up to believe that God can do anything. That God can give you riches if you want. I believe it because I can see and feel it. The members of our church sometimes prepares a feast for the lay preacher or Minister and all the congregation are invited. There may be as many as 50-60 people coming to a feast. It happens very often especially on white Sundays, Christmas and New Year. Most of them did not have jobs but they get all the food for the feast from their gardens, livestock, fishing or donations from relatives. They truly believe that God will provide.

It did create a certain special feeling in us children. We thought we were rich! We were eating like Kings very often! Our banquets included all the local delicacies, like whole roast pigs and imported sweets. We feel that we have a life of abundance. We did not have any money. We have no need for it, but we had abundance of food and we loved it as kids. It was only when I went to University in New Zealand that I realise that the bigger countries think we are poor! That our income per capita is lower than most countries and we could not afford the trappings of a modern society like cars, television and overseas holidays. But do you really need those things? Do cars, televisions and holidays make you happy? We often hear about millionaires who are always depressed or suicidal despite their wealth.

There are more important things in life than wealth. Wealth is good for living, but it will not always make you happy.

When we consider the purpose of our existence. Why are we on earth? Was it an accident of nature? That lightning hit the primordial soup and fused inanimate compounds to become single celled animals? Which can reproduce and gave rise to all living things through evolution? An accident of nature? I don't think that the obvious design of nature is an accident. Accidents are random, they are not in a pattern like evolution. Evolution is a definite design.

Why is earth where it is and the stars and galaxies where they are? Why can't we travel to any of the stars, visit other solar systems and galaxies? Isn't it because man cannot build a spacecraft that is fast enough to get there in our lifetime? It will take something like 190,000 years to fly to the nearest star in our quickest spaceship, and that is only 4 light years away!.

Man needs to think about this carefully. If he is not smart enough to build a spaceship to fly to the next star, then obviously he is not smart enough to interpret God's designs. I don't think it was the Big Bang that created the Universe, as some Scientists propose. But something similar with intelligent design. God put the solar systems around every star and stars in every galaxy. Man is just beginning to understand how things work in our bodies, on earth and in the universe.

Is the super being in us, God?. We know that sometimes certain people can perform miracles beyond our comprehension. It is impossible for the normal human being to do but it happens. Is it because those people are in touch with the Super Being or Energy Being inside them? They have learned to use its unlimited power? I think so. When we pray or perform affirmations or meditations we are trying to awaken the Energy Being in us to become one with us so we can use its super powers. Did Jesus know this? When he told the disciples how to pray? He send them the Holy Spirit which came like a "tongue of fire" according to the bible. It allowed the disciples to perform miracles in the name of Jesus.

The Roman Empire frowned upon the work of the early Christians and they were discriminated against. Tourists to-day can still visit the catacombs in Rome where the early Christians were buried. They were not allowed to bury their dead in Roman cemeteries so they dug up the earth and bury them underground. The Christian's great faith and the power of the Super or Energy Being within them won over the Roman Empire. The Holy Spirit. The word of God dominated over the swords and spears of the Roman soldiers. Rome is now the center of the largest of the Christian Churches, the Catholic Church.

Scientists can explain a lot of things about nature. We see miracles performed in the name of science everyday. The technology is so amazing to-day I can only say they are miracles. Modern medicine, radio, television, automobiles, telephones, computers, aircraft and so on. These are miracles performed by man. But where did man get his ideas? His inventions? His logic and inspiration? His enlightenment? Isn't it the Energy Being in all of us that is the creator? The all powerful, all knowing, all seeing Energy Being or Spirit in us? Isn't it the same being that brought down the Roman Empire in the name of Jesus Christ? The same being that came like a "tongue of fire" as the Holy Spirit? The same Super Being that guides your way every day and gives you everything that you need? If you take away that Super Being, what is left?

When we die our eyes look vacant and lifeless. It is opaque and unintelligent. Our bodies cannot move, then it starts to rot and decompose. Is it because the Energy Being that kept us alive has left our body? The Spirit has no more use for that body and left it? Then it becomes lifeless. The life giver is the Energy Being, Spirit or God? Just like a driver that turns off the ignition and left the car? The car, even though it is new, will start to rot or rust because there is no driver to turn it on, drive and maintain it.

Jesus has already taught us how to be in touch with the Super or Energy Being…through prayer. Some people also call it affirmations or meditation. If we need his help he is always there for us. The only time he is not with us is when we are dead. That means that he has left the earthly body. Some people believe that he takes on a new body like in reincarnation or he returns to God where he came from in the first place. Just like a little spaceship returning to the mother ship after its work is done.

So what is the point of it all? Are they aliens using the earth bodies to do their work on earth and when it's done they leave the body? And if their work is not finished, they come back in a new body? Are we just empty cars waiting for a driver? Are we just disposable suits to be discarded when the Super or Energy Being is finished with us?

Perhaps it is a bit of both.

If we look back at history. There are very few people who taught the general population things they need to know in order to live a life that is acceptable to society. Educating the population on everything from the word of God to how to cook food. It is still going on to-day. We are all learning things at different levels. And we are beginning to realise that sometimes we need help and a lot of people turn to prayer. To connect with the Super or Energy Being to extend a helping hand. Jesus.

Evangelists always ask the new converts to Christianity to ask Christ to enter their body and live his life in them. To become one with them. To help them understand God's design for them. It is a very good indication that indeed Christ was a Super or Energy Being. He was able to walk on water, raise the dead and do other miracles. When the disciples saw him walking towards them on the water, Peter asked Jesus if he can walk on water too. Jesus said yes. But Peter sank after 1 or 2 steps. His faith is not strong enough to hold him up on the water. He has doubts. He needs the Super or Energy Being to hold him up on the water but he does not know how to connect with it and how to use it through faith and prayer.

The world is rapidly changing through technology. Our kids will grow up learning through new technological tools like computers and super-computers, but will they learn what is most important? How to connect with the Energy Being in them. The one who is keeping them going? The one that drives them and gives them new ideas and thoughts? The one who keeps them alive? It is a new way of looking at how we live but perhaps it is something that we should take on consciously. Very often, it is the unconscious that drives us. For example, the heart beats by itself with no control from our conscious mind. Most of our other organs too are controlled by the brain unconsciously. Is it the Super or Energy Being controlling them? If it can perform miracles it must be. Because when it leaves the body, it is lifeless. It cannot move by itself!

If we look at the Universe, or just pictures of a cluster of galaxies and try to imagine how on earth they came into being. We will start to realise that it is indeed an intelligent design by an intelligent Super or Energy Being which is also present in all of us! We should be able to connect with it and the rest of the Universe because it is all seeing, all knowing and all powerful. It can do anything that you ask. All you have to do is connect with it through prayer, affirmations, meditations or whatever you want to call it. It seems that in all cases the Super Being does respond and grant your wishes, whatever you ask for. Then we will start to realise that we are not just empty cars waiting for a driver. The Super or Energy Being is our car and we are the drivers. The only difference is that our Super car can do anything. It can travel to the planets and galaxies. It can heal the sick and raise the dead! We just have to know how to drive it. Our super intelligent, all seeing, all knowing, all powerful car.

I should mention briefly here, that your brain actually programmes our genes through thoughts and words. We actually pass on a lot of our traits to our offspring that way. It is a kind of evolution, in a way, because as we become technologically advanced, our mind also programmes our genes to match or even surpass those advances. It is possible that the Super or Energy Being has a hand in it. Is it why man is progressively becoming smarter? By self-programming with assistance from his Inner Self? I think so.

We have power over our destiny in the flesh and in spirit. We can design our future generations by influencing the genes to make the necessary changes with help from the Super Energy Being in all of us. Our thoughts and words is the way to reach them both.

It does make mankind special. The problem is that most people tend to live their lives like empty cars, not knowing who to turn to or what to do most of the time when they run out of options. They just need a few seconds to connect to their Inner Self, Super or Energy Being to rescue them every time. It is not hard to do. Just say "Please help me" a hundred times to your Inner Self in affirmations. Or pray, "Jesus please help me"…and ask whatever you want. You will know that you will be alright if you have faith. Just like walking on water. If you do not believe, your inner self or Super Being or Energy Being will not be able to help you. Why? Because you are telling him, unconsciously, that you do not believe he can do anything for you. In other words you are cancelling your own requests by your own doubts. Don't forget it is all seeing, all knowing and all powerful. It will know your thoughts and what you feel in your heart.

In the next 5,000 million years, before the earth's final demise; when the sun runs out of fuel and grows into a red giant thus consuming and destroying the earth, man will have learned how to become a Super Being by connecting with the Energy Being inside. I have mentioned that man will be able to travel as an Energy Being, who is indestructible, to any part of the Universe. We no longer need the earth, we can settle anywhere we wish in any solar system or galaxy out there. Not in the flesh, which is perishable but as Super Energy Beings that exist forever. Perhaps that is what Christ promised in the New Testament. That we can live forever, if we become one with him? To become a Super Energy Being like him?

I think so.

CHAPTER 6. CONCLUSIONS

I believe it is time for us to write the 2nd Testament. The first being the New Testament. It should be a continuation of the Book of Revelations. There has been more miracles in the last 50 years then in the previous 1950 years. We have to write them down for future generations to read about.

When Jesus left he promised to send the Holy Spirit to guide his disciples and mankind. It came to the disciples like a tongue of fire. They were able to perform many miracles in the name of the Lord.

In modern times, everyday people can perform the same miracles, as in the bible. We can change water into wine by adding alcohol and flavours. We can raise the dead in the hospitals by passing an electric current through their hearts to restart it. We can fly through the air, walk on water, travel under the sea, send messages through the air to be received by radio and televisions thousands of kilometres away. We can talk to anyone around the world and see them at the other end on a screen. All those things are miracles.

The Holy Spirit has been guiding man for 2,000 years. Are all those modern miracles, revelations from the Holy Spirit? Believers think they are. All those miracles performed by man are revealed to him by the Holy Spirit. The Holy Spirit showed man how to turn water into wine, how to raise the dead, how to walk on water, travel through the air, manufacture medicine and goods and so on.

Without the Holy Spirit man will not be enlightened, he will probably never advance beyond the days of the bible. He would not have become the bright, miracle maker he is to-day. Do you believe this to be true?.

What about the non-believers? Why can they do the same things as everyone else?. The answer is in the sun and the rain. God gives life giving water and sunshine to all of mankind irrespective of their faith, color, wealth, background and so on. So does the Holy Spirit. It guides all of mankind, because the 2-3 billion Christians on earth have asked for it. They ask God in their prayers to help the sick, the governments and the people of the earth. And God has granted those requests....that is why there are more miracles now, by all of mankind, than before.

There are many things that man has yet to discover. How can he travel to other parts of the universe? His spaceship is so slow it will take more than 1,000 generations, living in a spaceship, to reach the nearest star at 4 light years away. Never mind the other billions of stars that are even up to hundreds of light years away.

Every star should have a solar system or planets revolving around it, according to current scientific theory. So every star, in theory, should have living beings in one of its revolving planets. But they are so far away, it is impossible to go there. Unless, we can discover something that only the Holy Spirit or Super Energy Being knows. How to travel at the speed of light or even faster than that. We can get to the nearest star in 4 years instead of 190,000 years. We can travel to anywhere in the universe. The problem is, we do not know how at the moment.

There are 100-400 billion stars and, at least, as many planets in our Galaxy, the Milky Way. Wikipedia.

I propose, that if we can recover our galactic memory we may discover that we are actually Energy or Spirit Beings that can travel at the speed of light, unaided in space. We are indestructible. We can take on many forms, human or other.

"Energy cannot be created or destroyed. It can only be changed from one form into another".

That is what we are. The only way to recover our galactic memory is to become one with the Super Energy Being himself. It is the Super Energy Being that knows where he has been in the last million years. Our flesh and earthly body was only born a few years before and it does not have the power and knowledge of the Super Energy Being.

The Holy Spirit or Super Energy Being will choose when and how to reveal it to us. Maybe sometime in the future when we learn a little bit more about ourselves and the universe we live in and how to become a Super Energy Being.

Man was created and "evolved" through intelligent design. Was it driven by the spirit? The immortal soul? Adam and Eve were punished from the Garden of Eden to live in pain and die forever. God the Son came and gave man God the Holy Spirit to guide and help him. Is that the Energy that drives us all? The Holy Spirit? It has been on Earth for 2,000 years. Since it came, soon after Christ left. It was like "a tongue of fire" the bible describes it.

It gave the disciples super powers. They were able to perform miracles too, and speak in "tongues". I believe it is the Super Energy Being working through them. They became one with it.

I suggest it is the same thing happening to-day. The evolution of man and ideas, with revelations from the Holy Spirit has helped to develop the world into what it is now. Man can recreate all the miracles in the bible and more. Man can even predict what is going to happen 5 billion years from now. The end of the earth, when the sun runs out of its fuel. Man has learned to become a miracle maker but has yet to become a Super Energy Being. If you were to travel back to the days of the bible and show them what you have to-day, they will probably worship you as a God. We have evolved into highly sophisticated beings with many technological advancements but not yet Super Beings.

When the earth is destroyed, man will have to move off somewhere. I propose that man will leave as a Spirit or Energy Being and populate other solar systems and beyond. The miracles man creates everyday are revelations from the ultimate power that drives him and the Universe, God the Holy Spirit. The Holy Spirit. The Immortal Soul. The Energy Being. We were created in his image. Us the Super Energy Beings in the making. We just don't know it yet.

Finally, I want to comment on the relationship between ancient and biblical knowledge and scientific explanations regarding god, evolution and man's destiny.

There are many religions and beliefs on earth, but they all seem to promote one thing and that is the "inner self, the spirit, the mind, enlightenment, everlasting life and god". There are many other references but they are all included in those six concepts.

It will take many books to discuss those six concepts, and many other authors have written about them, but I would like to comment on something that no one else has pointed out before. That is the relationship between your thoughts, your spoken words and your genetic being or makeup.

Have you ever wondered why your children sometimes behave and do things like you? Or your parents? We often say that our child has taken after grandpa, because he/she sometimes speak or behave like grandpa. How does that come about? I propose that when you think or speak, it is recorded by your brain like a computer records all information typed into it. That is why you remember what you said or thought about yesterday or even years before. It is recorded in your brain and **also your genetic makeup.** It is passed on to your children and descendants. Sometimes those traits are expressed sometimes they are not, in genetic terms.

I would like to expand on it a bit more.

When you speak, meditate or pray you are writing those information onto your genetic makeup. It is that process that will change things for you whether by improved physical traits, thoughts or offspring.

If you keep on repeating that message, it will be magnified by the brain and expressed immediately as in affirmations. Salesmen use affirmations to achieve something they want by repeating that goal a thousand times a day or so. They repeat it so many times that in a few days they believe in it with so much conviction that the customer too can feel the power of his words. His belief in his product convinced the customer to buy the product because the belief has been transferred to them through his presentation.

The same thing works with prayer.

When Christians pray they are convinced by the power of their words, which is also transferred to their listeners.

Non-believers can hear and feel the power of their words and convert to Christianity. The prayers are sometimes repeated so many times, like the Lord's prayer, that it actually creates the change through magnification and genetic effect. How did the ancients know about this? Through trial and error? Through divine intervention? As in the stories of the bible? It is said in the bible in the old testament that God… "effects his revenge on man down to the 3rd or 4th generation". Is it because the spoken "word of God is magnified and passed on in the genes to later generations"?.

Re-incarnation works in the same way.

The objective is to strive for enlightenment and purity of the heart or soul. Through meditation or prayer the genetic effect takes place by magnification in the brain and subsequent recording in the genes. Practitioners of reincarnation believe that when you achieve a certain level of enlightenment and purity you return to earth as a higher being, in the next life cycle or escape to the Cosmic Spirit.

We can extrapolate my proposal to include all things to do with the spoken words, thoughts and their genetic expression. Sorcery, witchcraft, black magic and so on.

They all work in the same way with Christian prayers, meditation or affirmations. How did the ancient practitioners of sorcery, black magic and so on knew?.

Through the power of the spoken words, its magnification by the brain and their recording and expression by the genes. Genes are all powerful because they control what you become. Your height, colour, number of teeth, eyes, nails, everything. Even how your body and brain works!

It is amazing! Isn't it? Now we can see or glimpse how it works. But who is in control of it all? Does our brain and genes work independently to turn us this way or that way? To make you feel good to-day and bad tomorrow? Evolutionary theory proposed by many Scientists to date suggest that it is selection or survival of the fittest that controls it. That only the good traits survive and the bad ones die off. But I venture to say, it is you and your spoken words that control it. Whether it is expressed through your genes depends on whether your brain magnifies it enough to be recorded. It is similar to one person versus a 1000 working on the same thing. You'll notice the effect quickly when there are 1000 people behind it versus one person.

But who controls you? That is my point. It is the Spirit Being, the Super Energy Being, God that controls you. Or controls the whole universe. We are still human made of bone, flesh and blood. Made by super beings much more intelligent than we are. We are being trained to be super beings ourselves. Our technology now will make us Gods in the eyes of St Peter and the apostles and the people of their day. In 1,000 million years who knows what we can do?

I propose that we should speed it up by programming ourselves through the spoken word, whether you pray, meditate or use other techniques. Magnify our good qualities so we can record them in our genes and pass them on to our descendants. Then we can become Super Energy Beings much quicker, perhaps like God himself.

I feel that I have touched on and explained every point that need to be explored to show that God is indeed energy itself. God is all seeing and all powerful. God is the Super Energy Being in all of us. The only way to be one with it is to ask him to be one with you and live through you. Then you will notice the power that comes through your spoken words. Then you will access your "galactic memory" and know where you have been in the last million years or since the beginning of the Universe.

Whether you choose to become one with God or not is up to you. But just like the rain and the sunshine, you too will also become a super being in the future. God will not deny you life giving rain or sunshine just because you don't believe or have lost your way. Do you Believe?.

BOOK 2

ALBERT EINSTEIN

"Great spirits have always encountered violent opposition from mediocre minds. The mediocre mind is incapable of understanding the man who refuse to bow blindly to conventional prejudices and chooses instead to express his opinions courageously and honestly".

Albert Einstein, 1940. Wiki-quotes.

Introduction.

This book is the second in this series on "creation and science". It is an attempt to collect existing information to explain our existence on earth. We cannot be an accident of nature. An evolutionary mutation in space and time which manifests itself in flesh and blood.

It is not a new idea. It is as old as time itself. The Higher Being is part of the Cosmic Spirit according to Hindu belief, for example. So this book will put together some ideas supported by literature to clarify exactly how the body works in relation to its true form, the cosmic self, the spirit, the Higher Being.

When I was at the University of Auckland, one of my Professors....John Morton...who was a "zoologist", always mention "evolution in the bible" during his invertebrate lectures. He was a man who spent years studying small animals on the beaches and reefs. He said something to the effect....that **they are so perfect and beautiful, they cannot be an accident of nature....it must be evolution in the biblical sense".** I think he means that evolution was inspired by divine beings. A creation that has no beginning or end. All living organisms evolving all the time into a better form.

That got me interested in the topic of "creation and science". What if.... science can be used to explain the spiritual world? The only problem, of course, is that we use "brick and mortar" analysis to analyse what cannot be seen. We have seen numerous TV documentaries trying to take photos of ghosts. We know ghosts are spirits, they are invisible to the naked eye. We cannot take photos of them!

Like the atoms or energy, we know spirits exist because we can sometimes see the "effect" but cannot see them. In the same TV documentaries looking for ghosts, gadgets that measure energy in the air can sometimes detect the "presence" of "something"......an energy being in the air..... but it cannot be photographed. They cannot see it. Only the energy meter can "see it". Just like a current meter detecting the presence of an electric current.

Energy is invisible to the human eye. We cannot take photos of energy. We can see its effects like light bulbs turned on by electricity, trees moved by the wind, planes flying in the air, humans running around, vehicles moving on the road and so on. The light and movements are caused by some form of energy, but we cannot see the energy itself.

Science has already explained the presence of energy. We know it exists. The total amount of energy in the universe is the same all the time. We cannot destroy it or create any more, but we can change it from one form into another. From solar energy into mechanical energy or heat energy and so on. Energy stored in petrol can be used to move vehicles, ships and planes. Energy stored in food can be used to move humans and living organisms. Energy stored in uranium can be exploded to do a lot of damage or harnessed to create electricity and mechanical energy.

Much of this was discussed in the first book. Man also changes from one form into another. From "flesh and blood" into a "spirit being". Man is made up of energy. The bible say that man was made in God's image. According to Hindus, when the body of flesh and blood dies the "spirit being" goes back to the "Cosmic Spirit".....in my view the totality of the energy in the Universe. This is probably the heaven that Christians talk about, being one with God. Muslims call it paradise. Buddhists, on the other hand, think achieving nirvana or "enlightenment" and escaping samsara or the endless cycle of births, deaths and rebirths driven by karma, is the goal of human existence. Perhaps they too join the cosmic spirit after being liberated from the sufferings of reincarnation?

Einstein did point out that mass is made of energy and therefore the whole universe is made up of energy.

We can safely conclude, that if God belongs in our universe, it must be made of energy. In that sense, the Cosmic Spirit is the total amount of energy in the universe, God.

In the Bible, when Jesus ascended to heaven he sent the Holy Spirit to empower the apostles. The Holy Spirit came like "the roar of a great wind" which looks like "tongues of fire". It entered the apostles and they were able to speak in other languages and perform miracles.

Modern man is also able to perform miracles in the name of science. In the last book, I concluded that the Holy Spirit must be the driver of all these miracles.

An attempt will also be made....in this book.... to explain how man develops with the "evolution of the spirit". Man's body is like a car. It cannot move by itself. It needs a driver. Man can drive a car, but he needs to learn how to drive and also gain experience to become a good driver. Similarly, our bodies cannot move by itself, it needs the "spirit" to drive it. We can tell how the spirit evolves throughout the life of the "man", as a baby, child, young adult and wise old man.

Would you rather that the Holy Spirit is your driver? If the Evil One is your driver you will find out quickly that he does not waste time. You will have so much trouble that your only solution is to run to God.

Throughout this book, I would like you to think of the meaning of these verses from the bible...

Luke 24:49-51

(Luke's version is similar to St John's).

"I am going to send you what my father has promised; but stay in the city until you have been clothed with the power from on high.

When he had led them out to the vicinity of Bethany, he lifted up his hands and blessed them and was taken up into heaven."

St Mark records it differently.

Mark 16 : 15-18

He said to them, "Go into all the world and preach the good news to all creation. Whoever believes and is baptized will be saved, but whoever does not believe will be condemned. And these signs will accompany those who believe; In my name they will drive out demons; they will speak in new tongues; they will pickup snakes with their hands; when they drink deadly poison it will not hurt them at all; they will place their hands on sick people and they will get well".

The promise of receiving the Holy Spirit and believing in Jesus Christ gives man the power to perform miracles in his name.

Acts 2: 1-4

"When the day of Pentecost came, they were all together in one place. Suddenly a sound like the blowing of a violent wind came from heaven and filled the whole house where they were sitting. They saw what seemed to be tongues of fire that separated and came to rest on each of them. All of them were filled with the Holy Spirit and began to speak in other tongues as the Spirit enabled them".

In the last book, I discussed "man the miracle maker" because Jesus had sent him the Holy Spirit which helped him to perform miracles....or "speak in other tongues".

The Holy Spirit is still with us to-day helping us to "raise the dead", "change water into wine", "walk on water" and so on. We have our own miracles to add to the ones in the bible....flying machines, computers, electricity and so on.

Hopefully, at the end of this book we have "connected the dots" between "man the flesh and blood" and "man the spirit"....an analysis of a spiritual kind....finding evidence of....The Higher Being, The Cosmic Spirit.

Chapter 1. The Beginning

When the male sperm enters the female egg, it passes its information and "fuses" with the egg to become a "fertilized egg" which began dividing furiously into an embryo. The embryo has begun to develop legs, arms, a torso and head. As it gets bigger, it became more and more complex with inner organs, brains, blood vessels, nerves and so on. Finally, in the ninth month when the baby is complete; it is born into the world as a separate person from its mother. Sometime between fertilization and being born, it learned or acquired the ability to exist by itself without being connected to its mother all the time.

Since birth the baby learns to eat, drink, laugh, make noises and speak, walk, run and play. At the age of 3, the toddler starts kindergarden and learns to sing, dance and socialize with other kids. Then he/she goes to Primary School, Intermediate School, High School then University where he/she is taught everything he/she needs to know to be a "successful adult".

It is interesting to note that although the spirit is in the child, yet the child still behaves like a child. If the spirit is born together with an infant surely the child will show the wisdom of the spirit or "The Higher Being" from an early age. The explanation, I believe, lies in the "car analogy"....the child's body. You can only do certain tasks with a car. A truck can carry a heavier load. A crane does different tasks. It is possible that the spirit, although it is the guide and mentor, can only do what is possible to the child. Therefore, if you are in a car, you cannot carry 100 people like a train. You can only perform like a car. This is a simplistic explanation but one that clearly demonstrates the point. A child can only do things that are possible to her/him at the particular age.

Furthermore, a child will have to learn to speak, to read and write and even to think logically. From an early age, parents can tell whether the child is normal or not.

Sometimes a child does not develop normally. There have been writers who point out that this abnormality is the affliction of the spirit not the body. In certain religions, it is called "karma" or the result of your previous sins. So it is the manifestation of the spirits "state of health" that is exhibited in the child. The symptoms are signs that all is not well with the spirit.

Karma - In Indian tradition is the principle that a person's actions have consequences that merit reward or punishment. Karma is the moral law of cause and effect by which the sum of a person's actions are carried forward from one life to the next , leading to an improvement or deterioration in that persons fate.

Penguin Encyclopedia.

When the spirit leaves the body, the body "dies". Eyes of dead people are opaque and show no life in it. You can tell the eyes of a dead person from a live one simply by looking at it. It is lifeless, it does not have the "spark" in the eyes of the living. In addition, the body cannot move by itself. A dead body is lifeless, no matter what age it is. How does the spirit make the body move? And why does it decide to leave a body?

Most Hindus believe that the spirit or soul is the true "self" of every person. It is eternal.

Hinduism. Wikipedia.

In my previous book , the energy from the sun and its flow through the food chain is discussed. There is also discussion of the "Energy Being" or Higher Being and its relation to energy. Einstein's equation $E = mc^2$ gives us a clue to this phenomenon. It means that the energy in a body is equal to its mass multiplied by the square of the velocity of light. Therefore, small amounts of mass can release large amounts of energy and large amounts of energy are required to create a small amount of mass. It follows, therefore, that mass and energy is one and the same thing. **The only conclusion we can draw is that the whole of the universe is made up of energy. God is Energy.**

"It follows from the special theory of relativity that mass and energy are different manifestations of the same thing.....a somewhat unfamiliar conception for the average mind. Furthermore, the equation E = mc², in which energy is put equal to mass, multiplied by the square of the velocity of light, showed that very small amounts of mass may be converted into a very large amount of energy and vice versa".

Albert Einstein, Theory of Relativity. Wiki-quotes.

(this theory was demonstrated experimentally by Cockcroft and Walton in 1932).

I have already discussed in "**God is Energy. Do you Believe**" that the spirit or Energy Being is part and parcel of God. The Higher Being is God. And God is the Universe because everything is made up of God himself or energy. Mass and Energy is one and the same thing.

The atom bomb is proof that E = mc² works. A small amount of mass or radioactive metal can release a huge destructive amount of energy.

Two atomic bombs were dropped on Hiroshima and Nagasaki in Japan, during World War II, by the Americans, caused so much terrible destruction that the Emperor and army of Japan surrendered immediately. Einstein was part of the team that worked to develop the atom bomb. It is called the atom bomb because the idea is to split the atoms of the radioactive fuel to release the energy stored in it. So much energy is released, all at once, that it has a huge amount of destructive power.

> Mass and Energy are one and the same thing. It follows that everything in the universe is energy. It is part and parcel of God.

This why the spirit can move the body because the spirit or God is energy. The energy that man uses came from the sun, trapped in the chloroplast of plants and stored in carbohydrate and nutrients in plants that man eats as rice, bread, vegetables and fruits to get his energy source. However, without the spirit it cannot use that energy source because the body would be lifeless. Is not God, the Spirit, the giver of life according to the scriptures?.

So what is the point of being born and grow into an adult? Then die and decompose? To be eaten by smaller animals and microbes? To live and learn subjects at school, find a job, start a family, save some money, buy a house and build up one's wealth when the only sure reward on earth is death? And you cannot take anything with you to the next life.....except perhaps your karma!.

You may also ask...what is the point of building cars and developing the technology to build and release better cars every year? Of building and developing all the other machinery and gadgets that man uses while he lives on earth? If the only sure way for it is the rubbish dump? Or being recycled into other goods?

I think the analogy makes sense.

Here's what Hinduism say about it;

This cycle of action, reaction, birth, death and rebirth is a continuum called samsara. The notion of reincarnation and karma is a strong premise in Hindu thought. The Bhagavad Gita states:

As a person puts on new clothes and discards old and torn clothes, similarly an embodied soul enters new material bodies, leaving the old bodies.

Wikipedia.

Evidence of the spirit also surface in the hospitals where "clinical death" patients talk about "floating in the air"!.

"When a person dies in the hospital....Doctors are able to revive him by passing an electric current through his heart. But is it his heart they are restarting? Or they are simply "returning the energy being within?".

There are many stories of clinical death in the hospitals. Of patients who have died for a few minutes...and they say that they have a sensation of looking down on their bodies as if they are floating in the air like a ghost! They watch the Doctors trying to revive them and....suddenly they wake up like they were asleep! Does the electric current attract the "spirit" back into the body with the energy boost?.

It may be worth studying such phenomenon as it is a "window" into the spirit world. Man might find out a lot more about his "inner self" or spirit.

Chapter 2. The Mind

The Mind is also referred to as the "Inner Self" and many other names. But if we look at the human body and all the functions of its different parts....the only conclusion is that the mind must be in the brain. It is the thinking and intuitive part of the brain. It "knows" a lot of things without even reading or studying the subject. Could it be that the "Inner Self" is "The Higher Being" himself ?. Giving you instructions and information that you need when you have not heard or seen it before? You just have a hunch that it could be right? Or you feel that it is the right one?.

When you talk or do things, it is recorded in your brain. You can recall the particular event and conversation that took place many years later. Most people remember them for life. What does that information do? Does the "brain" or "inner self" use it unconsciously to help you? Is that intuition or imagination? A total recollection and use of your memory?.

The memory does help you with your very survival. You avoid fires because you know it is hot. You don't jump off high buildings because you know you will get injured. You remember to eat and drink, wash yourself and do many other things to ensure your survival.

> "I believe in intuition and inspiration....at times I feel certain I am right while not knowing the reason. Imagination is more important than knowledge. For knowledge is limited, whereas imagination embraces the entire world, stimulating progress, giving birth to evolution. It is, strictly speaking, a real factor in scientific research."
>
> Albert Einstein, 1931. Wiki-quotes.

In learning and scientific research your brain uses the information stored to make conclusions and ask questions that ultimately give you the answers you are looking for. Does that mean your body and its parts are intelligent?

We all accept that the genes contain all the necessary information for the development of new life from male and female parents. But where does the genes get its information. How tall, hair, skin and eye colour, intelligence and so on? Can it be that our words and thoughts stored in the brain are used to write the genetic code into our genes? Can we influence the future generations through our words and deeds by writing what we want into the genetic code? A book can influence human kind for generations. The bible is one example. Do genes work in the same way?.

"You shall not make for yourself an idol in the form of anything in heaven above or of the earth beneath or in the waters below. You shall not bow down to them or worship them...for I, the Lord your God, am a jealous God, punishing the children for the sins of the fathers to the third and fourth generation of those who hate me, but showing love to a thousand generations, of those who love me and keep my commandments".

Commandment 2, Ten Commandments; Exodus 20 : 4.

The 2nd commandment in the Ten Commandments of Moses...given by God....suggest that God punish people for up to the 3rd and 4th generations....of those who "hate him"....and pray to other idols as Gods. Does this suggest "genetic coding"....that the words and deeds of the fathers will lead to their children's misfortunes? Or perhaps God strike them down with a bolt or lightning? Or endless cycles of rebirth....bad karma?

When the words and deeds are recorded in the brain, they can be recalled in a lifetime. If told to others or passed down as oral genealogy, they can be remembered for several generations. People do take action on these stories. But what about the brain or inner self? Is this karma?.

Karma translates literally as action, work, or deed, and can be described as the "moral law of cause and effect". According to Hindu literature an individual develops "impressions" from actions, whether physical or mental. A body more subtle than the physical one but less subtle than the soul, retains impressions, carrying them over into the next life, establishing a unique trajectory for the individual.

Hinduism, Wikipedia.

Hinduism believe that "impressions" developed from "actions"....probably spoken words or thoughts....are carried into the next generation and do influence the new babies being born. This information is not written in the genetic code...so where is it stored? It must be in the parent and passed to the offspring through the genes.

I once worked as a Salesman and one of the "success methods" we were taught is the power of affirmations. We were taught to write down what we want to happen in our sales presentation and recite it 100 times before making the presentation. I can say that it gave me a lot of confidence and conviction about my presentation. I can feel that my potential buyer is also convinced by my presentation, because through the affirmations, I convinced myself.

The same thing happens with Evangelists. They pray and prepare themselves for their sermon. I have heard some whose words were so powerful many people were converted. Some of the converts were crying and confessing their sins to God. Evangelists are well known for praying for "assistance" from God before they give their sermon. Does God give power ....through affirmations and prayer?".....to empower one to convert the listeners? Jesus did say......"ask and you shall receive".

The "inner self" must be the mechanism of control here. It records and act upon the words or the prayers. It is possible that the new cells produced in the body everyday are influenced in this way that their genetic makeup include the thoughts and words of that individual. Have you ever heard relatives say..."your grandson speaks and behaves like his father or grandfather?"....

This means that the genetic material passed on from the father is expressed in the kid's behaviour. But how did that genetic information got written into the genes in the first place? We all know it is a chemical process but we also know that feelings, words and thoughts do influence the production of chemicals in the body.

Feelings of happiness or anger influences what chemicals the body produce.

This maybe how we influence our genetic makeup. And this is probably what God refers to as his vengeance, down to the third and fourth generations. The sins and deeds of the fathers are passed on in their genes to the children. It may cause sickness, paralysis and other disabilities.

Karma of a very serious nature.

"The ultimate goal of life, referred to as moksha, nirvana or samadhi, is understood in several different ways: as the realization of one's union with God; as the realization of one's eternal relationship with God; realization of the unity of all existence; perfect unselfishness and knowledge of the Self; as the attainment of perfect mental peace; and as detachment from worldly desires. Such realization liberates one from samsara and ends the cycle of rebirth. Due to belief in the indestructibility of the soul, death is deemed insignificant with respect to the cosmic self. Thence, a person who has no desire or ambition left and no responsibilities remaining in life or one affected by a terminal disease may embrace death".

Hinduism. Wikipedia.

Chapter 3. Notes on the main Religions

I will briefly comment and display "summarized" information, from Wikipedia, on each of the major religions in this chapter to compare the similarities or differences in achieving the "state" of being "enlightened" and escaping suffering....returning to God or the Cosmic Spirit as believed by most of the major religions.

Hinduism is the oldest religion on earth. It is a complex culture of "dharma" or ethics and duties, "samsara" or the continuing cycle of birth, life, death and rebirth driven by "karma". The soul or spirit is eternal unless one wish to liberate oneself from samsara by abandoning all human desires or moksha....and return to the Cosmic Spirit.

Yoga is referred to as the right path. There are millions of people around the world who practice "yoga".

HINDUISM....summary.

"Hindus do not appear to have any differences with any other religion, welcoming all religions. Hinduism is not just a faith. It is the union of reason and intuition that cannot be defined, but is only to be experienced. Hinduism's tolerance to variations in belief and its broad range of traditions make it difficult to define as a religion according to traditional Western conceptions.

Unlike other religions in the World, the Hindu religion does not claim any one Prophet, it does not worship any one God, it does not believe in any one philosophic concept, it does not follow any one act of religious rites or performances; in fact, it does not satisfy the traditional features of a religion or creed. It is a way of life and nothing more.

Also, Hinduism does not have a single system of *salvation*, but consists of various religions and forms of religiosity. Some Hindu religious traditions regard particular rituals as essential for salvation, but a variety of views on this co-exist. Some Hindu philosophies postulate a theistic ontology of creation, of sustenance, and of the destruction of the universe, yet some Hindus are atheists, they view Hinduism more as philosophy than religion. Hinduism is sometimes characterised by a belief in reincarnation (samsara) determined by the law of karma and the idea that *salvation is freedom from this cycle of repeated birth and death.* Hinduism is therefore viewed as the most complex of all the living, historical world religions".

In Christianity it is the acceptance or belief in Christ who died on the cross to save the world from sin. John 3:16 gave this promise...."That whoever believeth in him shall not perish but have eternal life". It appears that there is a similarity that death is followed by being "born again" or rising from the dead. Eternal life can be "returning to the Cosmic Spirit or God" which is eternal.

"Hindu practices generally involve seeking awareness of God and sometimes also seeking blessings from deities.

Therefore, Hinduism has developed numerous practices meant to help one think of divinity in the midst of everyday life. *Mantras* are invocations, praise and prayers that through their meaning, sound, and chanting style help a devotee focus the mind on holy thoughts or express devotion to God/the deities. Many devotees perform morning ablutions at the bank of a sacred river while chanting.

Hinduism grants absolute and complete freedom of belief and worship. Hinduism conceives the whole world as a single family that defies the one truth, and therefore it accepts all forms of beliefs and dismisses labels of distinct religions which would imply a division of identity. Hence, Hinduism is devoid of the concepts of apostasy, heresy and blasphemy.

Samsara provides ephemeral pleasures, which lead people to desire rebirth so as to enjoy the pleasures of a perishable body. However, escaping the world of samsara through moksha is believed to ensure lasting happiness and peace. It is thought that after several reincarnations, an *atman* (enlightened spirit) eventually seeks unity with the *cosmic spirit* (God)."

Hinduism is based on "the accumulated treasury of spiritual laws discovered by different persons in different times". The scriptures were transmitted orally in verse form to aid memorization, for many centuries before they were written down. Over many centuries, sages refined the teachings and expanded the canon. In post-Vedic and current Hindu belief, most Hindu scriptures are not typically interpreted literally. More importance is attached to the ethics and metaphorical meanings derived from them. Most sacred texts are in Sanskrit".

The following is a summary of the Buddhist idea of how man will find peace and escape reincarnation and sufferings of the flesh on earth.

BUDDHISM...summary.

"Buddhism is a nontheistic religion that encompasses a variety of traditions, beliefs and practices largely based on teachings attributed to Siddhartha Gautama, *who is commonly known as the Buddha, meaning "the awakened one"*. According to Buddhist tradition, the Buddha lived and taught in the eastern part of the Indian subcontinent sometime between the 6th and 4th centuries BCE. He is recognized by Buddhists as an awakened or enlightened teacher who shared his insights to help sentient beings end their suffering through the *elimination of ignorance* and craving *by way of understanding* and with the ultimate goal of attainment of the sublime state of *Nirvana* (enlightenment)".

Buddhism, unlike Christianity and Hinduism, aim to
eliminate ignorance through understanding and
achieving "Nirvana" or "Awakening" or
"Enlightenment"; thus escaping samsara...the cycle
of births and rebirths. Perhaps through "abandoning
all worldly desires".

Buddhism is practiced primarily in Asia, estimates of
Buddhists worldwide vary significantly depending on the
way Buddhist adherence is defined. Estimates range from
350 million to 1.6 billion, with 350–550 million the most
widely accepted figure. Figures for Christianity could be
as high as 2-3 billion and 1.5-2 billion for Hindus.
Moslems also have about 1-2 billion members.

"Buddhist schools vary on the exact nature of the path to
liberation, the importance and canonicity of various
teachings and scriptures, and especially their respective
practices. The foundations of Buddhist tradition and
practice are the Three Jewels: the Buddha, the Dharma
(the teachings), and the Sangha (the community). Taking
"refuge in the triple gem" has traditionally been a
declaration and commitment to being on the Buddhist
path, and in general distinguishes a Buddhist from a

non-Buddhist.

The evidence of the early texts suggests that Siddhārtha Gautama was born in a community that was on the periphery, both geographically and culturally, of the northeastern Indian subcontinent in the 5th century BCE. After the birth of young prince Gautama, an astrologer named Asita visited the young prince's father—King Śuddhodana—and prophesied that Siddhartha would either become a great king or renounce the material world to become a holy man, depending on whether he saw what life was like outside the palace walls. Śuddhodana was determined to see his son become a king, so he prevented him from leaving the palace grounds. But at age 29, despite his father's efforts, Gautama ventured beyond the palace several times. In a series of encounters—known in Buddhist literature as the four sights—he learned of the suffering of ordinary people, encountering an old man, a sick man, a corpse and, finally, an ascetic holy man, apparently content and at peace with the world. These experiences prompted Gautama to abandon royal life and take up a spiritual quest.

Gautama first went to study with famous religious teachers of the day, and mastered the meditative attainments they taught. But he found that they did not provide a permanent end to suffering, so he devoted himself to meditation, through which he discovered what Buddhists call the Middle Way, a path of moderation between the extremes of self-indulgence and self-mortification.

Gautama was now determined to complete his spiritual quest. At the age of 35, he famously sat in meditation under a sacred fig tree — known as the Bodhi tree — in the town of Bodh Gaya, India, and vowed not to rise before achieving enlightenment. After many days, he finally destroyed the fetters of his mind, thereby liberating himself from the cycle of suffering and rebirth, and arose as a fully enlightened being . Soon thereafter, he attracted a band of followers and instituted a monastic order. Now, as the Buddha, he spent the rest of his life teaching the path of awakening he had discovered, travelling throughout the northeastern part of the Indian subcontinent, and died at the age of 80 (483 BCE) in Kushinagar, India".

Within Buddhism, samsara is defined as the continual repetitive cycle of birth and death that arises from ordinary being's grasping and fixation on the self and experiences. Specifically, samsara refers to the process of cycling through one rebirth after another within the six realms of existence,[a] where each realm can be understood as physical realm or a psychological state characterized by a particular type of suffering. Samsara arises out of ignorance and is characterized by suffering, anxiety and dissatisfaction.

Karma - In Buddhism karma is the force that drives samsara—the cycle of suffering and rebirth for each being. Good, skillful deeds and bad, unskillful actions produce "seeds" in the mind that come to fruition either in this life or in a subsequent rebirth. The avoidance of unwholesome actions and the cultivation of positive actions is called "ethical conduct". In Buddhism, karma specifically refers to those actions of body, speech or mind that spring from mental intent and bring about a consequence or fruit, or result.

Some karma "maybe just part of the universe" and similar to forgiveness of sin, negative karma, can be "forgiven" through recitation of special scriptures....or prayers. Negative karma is said to cause the cycle of suffering which results from births, deaths and rebirths. Escaping samsara is the ultimate "salvation"....which is similar to Hinduism.

"Rebirth refers to a process whereby beings go through a succession of lifetimes as one of many possible forms of sentient life, each running from conception to death. *Buddhism rejects the concepts of a permanent self or an unchanging, eternal soul, as it is called in Hinduism and Christianity.* According to Buddhism there ultimately is no such thing as a self independent from the rest of the universe. Buddhists also refer to themselves as the believers of the "anatta" doctrine. Rebirth in subsequent existences must be understood as the continuation of a dynamic, ever-changing process of "dependent arising",

86

determined by the laws of cause and effect (karma) rather than that of one being, transmigrating or incarnating from one existence to the next".

The Buddha's teachings is based on the Four Noble Truths, regarded as central to the teachings of Buddhism, and are said to provide a conceptual framework for Buddhist thought. These four truths explain the nature of suffering, anxiety, unfulfilled, its causes, and how it can be overcome. The four truths are:

1. The truth of suffering, anxiety, being unfulfilled (dukkha).

2. The truth of their origin

3. The truth of their cessation

4. The truth of the path leading to their cessation

The obvious suffering of physical and mental illness, growing old, and dying. The anxiety or stress of trying to hold onto things that are constantly changing. A subtle dissatisfaction pervading all forms of life, due to the fact that all forms of life are changing, impermanent and without any inner core or substance. On this level, the term indicates a lack of satisfaction, a sense that things never measure up to our expectations or standards.

The second truth is that the origin of dukkha can be explained as craving conditioned by ignorance. On a deeper level, the root cause of dukkha is identified as ignorance of the true nature of things. The third noble truth is that the complete cessation of dukkha is possible, and the fourth noble truth identifies a path to this cessation.

Nirvana

Nirvana means "cessation", "extinction" of craving and ignorance and therefore suffering and the cycle of involuntary rebirths (samsara), "extinguished", "quieted", "calmed"; it is also known as "Awakening" or "Enlightenment" in the West. The term for anybody who has achieved nirvana, including the Buddha, is arahant.

Awakening of arahants is more commonly translated into English as "enlightenment", a meaning synonymous to nirvana, using only some different metaphors to describe the experience, which implies the extinction of greed, craving, hate, aversion and delusion.

The Mahayana tradition separated them and considered that nirvana referred only to the elimination of craving (passion and hatred), with the resultant escape from the cycle of rebirth. This interpretation ignores the third fire, delusion: the extinction of delusion is of course in the early texts identical with what can be positively expressed as gnosis, Enlightenment.

Buddhas

According to Buddhist traditions a Buddha is a fully awakened being who has completely purified his mind of the three poisons of desire, aversion and ignorance. A

Buddha is no longer bound by Samsara and has ended the suffering which unawakened people experience in life. Therefore, Siddhartha Gautama was not the only Buddha. The history shows a list of 28 Buddhas and also many Buddhas of celestial, rather than historical, origin.

The following is a summary of the "essence" of the religion of Islam. It is slightly different in that emphasis is on the "resurrection of the body" rather than "rebirth" of the spirit. However, the Muslims believe that, after death, they will "enter" paradise if they live life according to the teachings of the prophet Muhammad.

ISLAM....summary.

"Islam is a monotheistic and Abrahamic religion articulated by the Quran (Koran), considered by its adherents to be the word of God (Allah) and by the teachings and normative example of Muhammad , considered by them to be the last prophet of God. An adherent of Islam is called a Muslim. Muslims believe that God is one and incomparable and *the purpose of existence is to worship God.* Muslims also believe that *Islam is the complete and universal version of a faith that was revealed before many times throughout the world, including through Adam, Noah, Abraham, Moses and Jesus, whom they consider prophets.*They maintain that the previous messages and revelations have been partially misinterpreted or altered over time, but consider the Arabic Quran to be both the unaltered and the final revelation of God. Religious concepts and practices

89

include the five pillars of Islam.... They are (1) the shahadah (creed), (2) daily prayers (salat), (3) almsgiving (zakah), (4) fasting during Ramadan and (5) the pilgrimage to Mecca (hajj) at least once in a lifetime.

Islam believers demonstrate submission to God by serving God, following his commands, and rejecting polytheism. *Muslims and Jews repudiate the Christian doctrine of the Trinity and divinity of Jesus, comparing it to polytheism.* In Islam, God is beyond all comprehension and Muslims are not expected to visualize God, the most common Allah..."The Compassionate" or "The Merciful". Allah is the term with no plural or gender used by Muslims and Arabic-speaking Christians and Jews to refer to God".

The Quran, and the Islamic holy books are the records which most Muslims believe were dictated by God to various prophets. *The Quran is divided into 114 chapters, which combined, contain 6,236 verses.* The chronological order are primarily concerned with ethical and spiritual topics. Muslims identify the prophets of Islam as those humans chosen by God to be his messengers. The Quran mentions the names of numerous figures considered prophets in Islam, including Adam, Noah, Abraham, Moses and Jesus, among others. Muslims believe that God finally sent Muhammad as the last prophet to convey the divine message to the whole world.

Similar to Christianity and Hinduism , Muslims believe in the *"judgement and day of resurrection"*. They believe the time is preordained by God but unknown to man, but the emphasis is on a bodily resurrection...not a spiritual one....

"Ritual prayers must be performed five times a day. The prayers are done with the chest in direction of Mecca though in the early days of Islam, they were done in direction of Jerusalem. A mosque is a place of worship for Muslims. "Zakāt" is giving a fixed portion of accumulated wealth by those who can afford it to help the poor or needy and for those employed to collect Zakat. Fasting, from food and drink (among other things) must be performed from dawn to dusk during the month of Ramadhan. The pilgrimage, called the ḥajj has to be done during the Islamic month of Dhu al-Hijjah in the city of Mecca. Every able-bodied Muslim who can afford it must make the pilgrimage to Mecca at least once in his or her lifetime, following the foot steps of Abraham..... recounting the steps of Abraham's wife, while she was looking for water for her son Ismael in the desert before Mecca developed into a settlement".

A Brief History of Islam

In Muslim tradition, Muhammad (c. 570 – June 8, 632) is viewed as the last in a series of prophets. During the last 22 years of his life, beginning at age 40 in 610 CE, according to the earliest surviving biographies, Muhammad reported revelations that he believed to be from God conveyed to him through the archangel Gabriel. The content of these revelations, known as the Quran, was memorized and recorded by his companions.

During this time in Mecca, Muhammad preached to the people imploring them to abandon polytheism and to worship one God. Although some converted to Islam, Muhammad and his followers were persecuted by the leading Meccan authorities. The Arab tribes in the rest of Arabia then formed a confederation and during the Battle of the Trench besieged Medina intent on finishing off Islam. Muhammad was victorious in the nearly bloodless Conquest of Mecca, and by the time of his death in 632 (at the age of 62) he united the tribes of Arabia into a single religious polity.

The largest denomination in Islam is Sunni Islam, which makes up 75%–90% of all Muslims. While the Sunnis believe that a Caliph should be elected by the community.

Rejecting the legitimacy of the previous Muslim caliphs. Shia Islam has several branches.

There are also other smaller groups. Sufism is a mystical-ascetic approach to Islam that seeks to find divine love and knowledge through direct personal experience of God. By focusing on the more spiritual aspects of religion, Sufis strive to obtain direct experience of God by making use of "intuitive and emotional faculties" that one must be trained to use.

A comprehensive 2009 demographic study of 232 countries and territories reported that 23% of the global population, or 1.57 billion people, are Muslims. Of those, it is estimated over 75–90% are Sunni and 10–20% are Shia with a small minority belonging to other sects. Approximately 57 countries are Muslim-majority, and Arabs account for around 20% of all Muslims worldwide.

The majority of Muslims live in Asia and Africa.

Approximately 62% of the world's Muslims live in Asia, with over 683 million adherents in Indonesia, Pakistan, India, and Bangladesh. In the Middle East, non-Arab countries such as Turkey and Iran are the largest Muslim-majority countries; in Africa, Egypt and Nigeria have the most populous Muslim communities. Most estimates indicate that the People's Republic of China has approximately 20 to 30 million Muslims.

Chapter 4. Enlightenment

> "The Compact Oxford Dictionary describes "Enlightenment" as "the gaining of knowledge and understanding". It was also a movement in Europe in the 17th and 18th century emphasizing reason and individualism rather than tradition".

Enlightenment can be achieved through study of the scriptures or attaining of knowledge through school and research. Buddhist monks spent a lifetime studying the old teachings and practicing meditation. In order to reach that higher goal of becoming all wise and knowing the "right path", one must achieve the state of nirvana or being "awakened" or "enlightened".

Many religious people also practice and study their old scriptures to gain enlightenment. In the Christian bible, Luke 24 :44-47 talks about *Jesus opening the disciples eyes* so that they can understand what has been written about him in the scriptures. The disciples reached the state of being "enlightened" when Jesus opened their eyes. They understand what has been written in the Law of Moses and by the prophets and in the Psalms.

Luke 24 : 44-47.

"This is what I told you while I was still with you. Everything must be fulfilled that was written about me in the Laws of Moses, the prophets and the Psalms. Then he opened their minds so they could understand the Scriptures. He told them,

"This is what is written: The Christ will suffer and will rise from the dead on the third day, and repentance and forgiveness of sin will be preached in his name to all nations, beginning at Jerusalem.

It appears that enlightenment is a state of mind. Jesus simply "*opened their minds*" so they can understand the scriptures and he also sent the Holy Spirit to change them from ordinary men into Super Beings. They were able to "heal the sick and drive out demons in the name of the Lord".

Jesus, from all accounts, was the "enlightened one" the "Super Being" or "The Higher Being" that we all should be....but we need to be "awakened".

In Mark 6 : 49 - 50

"But when they saw him walking on the lake, they thought he was a ghost. They cried out because they all saw him and were terrified".

In St Matthews account....St Peter asked Jesus if he can walk on the water too, *but he sank as soon as he took a few steps on the water.* He did not have enough faith to hold him up in the water. He began worrying about sinking rather than "doing the walking"....that Jesus commanded him to do. *This is the difference between an awakened being and one that is not. An awakened being can walk on water.*

This is the problem with becoming enlightened, man does not have the "power of faith" to hold him up in the water.

He knows that he cannot walk on the water. Even though a man will claim he has great faith....still he knows he cannot walk on water. It is only the power of the Holy Spirit that will allow him to walk on water, heal the sick and drive out demons. The Holy Spirit allows him to become a "Super Being" by bringing out the power of the "inner self"..."The Higher Being" that is present in all of us......*by being "awakened" like the Buddha. Enlightened.*

Study does give a man a certain amount of knowledge. Einstein suggested that a man also needs imagination, intuition and fantasy in order to become enlightened. To reach that higher goal of knowledge that can only be achieved when *"God opens one's eyes to know what is hidden"* from all mortals. We can refer to Einstein as an "enlightened man". He was able to find the truth about energy or what God wants him to find. **A discovery so great that Albert Einstein is revered by all scholars and people who know of his work.** He is among the immortals like Muhammad, Buddha and the Gods.

Science has many more "universal truths" that man has uncovered. Man has become a miracle maker, through the power of the Holy Spirit. Any man can turn water into wine by adding alcohol and flavours, any man can walk on water using technology, doctors heal the sick and raise the dead.

We know that since the Holy Spirit came "like the roar of a great wind" and took over the apostles....who became "awakened" or "enlightened". They spoke in other languages and performed miracles.

Through the promise of the Holy Spirit, anyone who believes in Jesus Christ becomes "awakened". They are the miracle makers of to-day, the 20th century. But the revelations made by the Holy Spirit is so far reaching that education can also "awaken" mankind. God has chosen to enlighten mankind if they choose to embrace it. Just like his miracles that come from the life giving sunshine and the rain.

God does not choose who receives life giving sunshine and water....it is a gift for all of mankind.

Just like being enlightened by education.

Chapter 5. The Promised Kingdom

Science sometimes talks about parallel universes that exist together with ours. Any of those parallel universes could be the paradise often talked about in the religions of the world. There are certain "gates" that we go through to enter. There can be unlimited numbers of parallel universes, but like Einstein say that even though his positive knowledge was great....he truly values his ability to fantasize...it was a great tool in his scientific research, being able to imagine the solution.

There is a story about St Peter being the "Gate Keeper" into the Kingdom of Heaven...and it is entirely possible it is a kind of parallel universe.

The whole of the Christian faith is the promise made in **John 3:16..."That God so loved the world that he gave his only begotten son....that whoever believeth in him shall not perish but have everlasting life"**.

Most Christians believe that this refers to the soul. It is man's soul or spirit that will live forever. Not his human form of flesh and blood. Again, we encounter the idea of "The Higher Being". To have everlasting life and live forever, it only means that the soul, spirit or the "Higher Being" is a super being capable of powers beyond human comprehension.

In the book of **Acts 2: 1-4** the Holy Spirit became one with the apostles;

"When the day of Pentecost came, they were all together in one place. Suddenly a sound like the blowing of a violent wind came from heaven and filled the whole house where they were sitting. They saw what seemed to be tongues of fire that separated and came to rest on each of them. All of them were filled with the Holy Spirit and began to speak in other tongues as the Spirit enabled them".

And they were able to perform miracles in the name of Jesus. Consider the case of the cripple outside the temple gates. Peter and John were entering the temple and a crippled man asks them for money.

Acts 3: 1-8.

One day Peter and John were going up to the temple at the time of prayer...at 3 in the afternoon. Now a man crippled from birth was being carried to the temple gate called Beautiful, where he was put everyday to beg from those going into the temple courts. When he saw Peter and John about to enter, he asked them for money. Peter looked straight at him as did John. Peter said, "Look at us!". So the man gave them his attention, expecting to get something from them.

Then Peter said, "Silver or gold I do not have, but what I have I will give you. In the name of Jesus Christ of Nazareth, walk". Taking him by the right hand, he helped him up, and instantly the man's feet and angles became strong . He jumped to his feet and began to walk.

What the cripple got was far more precious than a silver or gold coin. God through the Holy Spirit and St Peter gave him his freedom. His ability to walk again. There were many other miracles performed by the apostles in the name of Jesus....with the help of the Holy Spirit.

All the major religions have one goal in common. *"Man returning to the Cosmic Spirit"* as the Hindus put it. The Cosmic Spirit is the essence of God...and I say...the energy driving the universe. It appears that the promised Kingdom is God himself. God is the Universe...but is it this one or a parallel one? But then God is all powerful and all encompassing that anything is possible.

When every person dies, all major religions agree they will return back to God; whether they are punished through karma and samsara as the Hindus and Buddhists believe or return in their human body is irrelevant. I think we all agree that God is the Cosmic Spirit, the Universe and he is all knowing and all powerful.

Jesus did say that when Christians are "born again" and accept him as their saviour he becomes one with them. He lives his life through them. They become "*one with GOD*". It is very similar to returning to the Cosmic Spirit as believed by Hindus. They are saved and will enter the promised kingdom....perhaps the Cosmic Kingdom! The Kingdom of Heaven, a parallel universe.

Anything is possible.

The Cosmic self is eternal. It has no beginning or end. *Hindus belief that the Cosmic self is the "true-self"*....the human body being just a punishment....demoted to the

100

endless cycle of birth, death and rebirth until one finds redemption through Christ, nirvana or liberation from karma.

CHAPTER 6. CONCLUDING COMMENTS

The bible refers to "eternal death" or what Jesus call "condemnation". It is becoming clear that it means the total and complete loss of man "the flesh and blood". Only man "the spirit" will survive. When man "the flesh and blood" dies his soul or spirit returns to the Cosmic Spirit according to Hinduism; or it ascends to heaven according to Christians. Only the Muslims believe that man "the flesh and blood" will arise from the dead, a gift from Allah to believers of the prophet Muhammad.

The marriage of science and creation has created some interesting questions but it also demonstrates that the world is "interconnected". The material and the spiritual world are mutually inclusive. *Scientists call them "parallel universes".* You can enter these parallel universes through "gates". Do all religions have their own parallel universe? Can the "collective mind" create a new "parallel universe"?.

The Christian religion talks about St Peter as the "Gate Keeper"...and Jesus did say that "Peter is the rock" and on that rock he will build his church. Is St Peter the gate keeper to the parallel universe we go to when we die? Heaven?.

Einstein was thankful for his ability to fantasize because it enabled him to "imagine the solutions" to the hard Scientific questions he faced. The discovery of $E = mc^2$ is a discovery so great it does lend good reason to the use of fantasy or imagination to solving "impossible" problems....scientific or not.

There are clues to the existence of "The Higher Being" in us all. The Spirit. Sometimes it is the unconscious mind that gives us the answers. People often speak of things they are not aware or know of. Simply a "slip of the tongue", but if you think about it; nothing you do is accidental. It is all controlled by your "mind"...The Higher Being.

In the Christian belief, being "born again" is accepting Jesus Christ died on the cross to save the world and forgive their sins. When you accept Jesus as your saviour he will enter your body and become you. He will live your life for you. This is God's way of bringing you back to him. Returning to the Cosmic Spirit ....in Hindu belief.

It is becoming clear *"that man cannot live by bread alone"*. Man needs the spirit or he will die. When the **Higher Being** leaves him his body becomes lifeless and "returns to the earth where it came from".

Literature Cited....

1. The Holy Bible - Authorized King James Version

2. The Holy Bible - New International Version

3. Penguin Encyclopedia

4. Compact Oxford Dictionary

5. Wiki-quotes - Internet Free Encyclopedia

6. Wikipedia - Internet Free Encyclopedia.

About the author...

Semisi Pone is a graduate of the University of Auckland. He graduated in 1985 with a BSc and a MSc (Hons) in 1989. He has worked overseas in Tonga as a Plant Pathologist and Senior Plant Virologist, the University of the South Pacific in Samoa as a Fellow, the South Pacific Commission in Fiji as an Advisor and Head of the Plant Protection Services and also did some work for the United Nations (FAO, Rome) in one of its expert panels and Regional Plant Protection Organisation technical meetings.

He has also worked in various places and jobs in Auckland. He is interested in the topic of "man's mortality" and the "immortal soul" hence this book. He believes that it is something "worth discussing around the dinner table".

He also writes books in other genre mainly humour, poetry, fiction, non-fiction, stories for kids, science and anything else that he is interested in.

Semisi Pone has published more that 70 books and ebooks in New Zealand and on the internet. You can view these books in Blurb.com, Apple.com , Amazon.com and Wheelers.co.nz bookstores.